LIFE IS

Rivian Marcus
Workshops for Living

Book Design by Tara Marcus | Book Layout by Hedy Sirico

© Copyright 2004. All rights reserved.

LIFE IS A FOUR-LETTER WORD

Dedicated to:

Hesh
(The wind beneath my wings)

and

To My Children &
My Children's Children

LIFE IS A FOUR-LETTER WORD

ACCEPT your reality, let go of "should have" "could have" "would have". Be proactive with your life and get on with doing what needs to be done in order to heal yourself and move on.

BE wary of "easy fixes" and the "easy way out". "Short cuts" are apt to "short change" your life. If it is worth doing, it is worth doing right!

CANCEL! CANCEL!

all negative thoughts. Negative thoughts bring negative situations into your life. We are like magnets...attracting what we give off.

LIFE IS A FOUR-LETTER WORD

**DECISIONS** have to be made! Do not sit on the fence and hope for someone to rescue you. Indecision does not move you forward... action does.

EXTEND yourself. Go the extra steps to do things with care and integrity. There are great emotional rewards for doing things well.

FOCUS on the positives (large or small) in your life. Make yourself aware of the things in your life that do go well. Learn to "accent the positive".

GET GOING... do not sit around and wring your hands. Do anything, no matter how trivial. Being occupied is the best medicine for what ails you. Make a call, write a note, bake cookies. Use your negative energy to do something worthwhile.

HELP someone who needs your comfort and attention, and you might realize that you don't have it so bad.

LIFE IS A FOUR-LETTER WORD

INVITE someone in for coffee and conversation. You need never be alone or lonely.

LIFE IS A FOUR-LETTER WORD

JUGGLE your schedule to make time for yourself. Your well-being and the well-being of your loved ones depend on your strength.

LIFE IS A FOUR-LETTER WORD

KICK the habit of being judgmental. You do not really know what is going on in someone else's life. Try giving them the "benefit of the doubt."

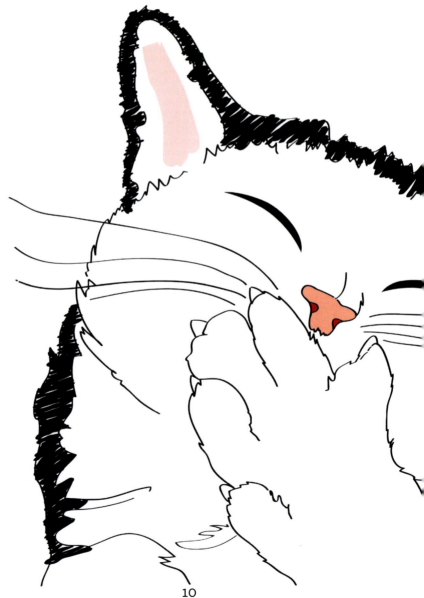

LIFE IS A FOUR-LETTER WORD

LIVE life to the fullest! **LOVE** yourself and your dear ones unconditionally. **LAUGH** as much as you possibly can. **LIGHTEN UP** and free yourself from old habits. **LET GO** of what you no longer need in your life.

LIFE IS A FOUR-LETTER WORD

MAKE someone happy. If you focus on another's well-being and happiness, you may find that you have found your own happiness.

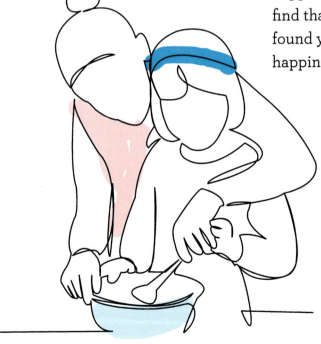

NOTICE the existence of nature...cloud formations, the moon & stars. Take time to "smell the roses"...or the smell of the ocean. Become more aware of the beauty there is in this world.

OPEN your mind, heart and soul to receive new and exciting opportunities into your life. Drop the old habits and become creative with your future.

PRACTICE saying "NO" at the appropriate times. Say "SORRY, I cannot do that now" and do not engage in apologies and excuses.

LIFE IS A FOUR-LETTER WORD

QUESTION your motives and your priorities. You may find that you are making decisions that are not necessarily in your best interest.

LIFE IS A FOUR-LETTER WORD

RELAX and take several breaths before an angry encounter. Is it really necessary to win an argument...prove a point... be right? Sometimes saying "OK" can be a real WIN-WIN solution for you!

LIFE IS A FOUR-LETTER WORD

SAVOR the good moments, no matter how mundane. Enjoy the creature comforts that you may be taking for granted…a comfortable bed…clean sheets…a hot shower…fresh coffee… air conditioning in the summer…heat in the winter.

LIFE IS A FOUR-LETTER WORD

TREAT people kindly. Your smile and good word may go a long way to ease the strain and pain that a waitress or a person at the check out counter may be experiencing. Would you want to change places with them?

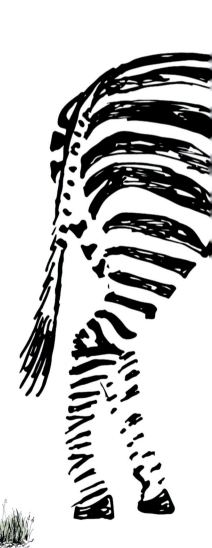

USE your time wisely. It is a very precious commodity. Never say "I have to kill some time." Celebrate every precious moment.

VARY your routine. Do something different and enjoyable. Get out of your rut. Go to a museum, the zoo, a concert, a lecture, a book store. Turn off the TV and challenge yourself to come up with some new ideas.

WHAT is your purpose in life? Why are you here now and what can you do to make your little corner of life a better place in which to live? Embrace silence and see what you come up with. You might surprise yourself.

X-RAY your lifestyle. Is it a healthy and sensible approach to living well? If not... change your eating habits...exercise...get more rest. Invest in your own well-being.

LIFE IS A FOUR-LETTER WORD

LIFE IS A FOUR-LETTER WORD

YOU are a good person. Learn to love and accept who and what you are. If you respect yourself, others will also respect you.

LIFE IS A FOUR-LETTER WORD

ZERO in on Life!!!
And live it to the fullest.
This is not a "dress
rehearsal", so make the
most of it.

LIFE IS A FOUR-LETTER WORD

NOTES

Your Own Thoughts For Living

LIFE IS A FOUR-LETTER WORD

NOTES

Your Own Thoughts For Living

NOTES

Your Own Thoughts For Living

NOTES

Your Own Thoughts For Living

ABOUT THE AUTHOR

Rivian Marcus grew up in a Jewish neighborhood in South Philadelphia in the 1930's. Her father, Harry, owned a bakery. Her loving mom Esther emigrated from Eastern Europe under very difficult circumstances.

Rivian's spiritual life started to take root in the 1970's. She was trained in Transcendental Meditation and Jose Sylva's Mind process. Her path and a cancer diagnosis led her to study and practice the work of Louise Hay, Caroline Myss and Dr. Bernie Siegel.

Rivian has always been a deeply caring soul. She and her husband became Para-chaplains in hospitals and led Jewish services in senior living facilities for 20 years. Rivian started to lead workshops to help people find more peace, to think positively and find order in chaos. Along with Heshy, her devoted husband of 70 years, Rivian spent more than a decade traveling the world on cruise ships leading her highly regarded Workshops for Living. Professionally, Rivian, along with her husband, ran a successful Interior Design business.

Life Is A Four-Letter Word™ came to Rivian in the middle of the night. She sat down and wrote this guide for living in one sitting. Her simple principles introduce us to profound and transformative practices that will help each of us live today more fully, peacefully and kindly.

Should you get to meet Rivian, ask her for one of her hug cards. She has spent a lifetime giving those around her, one giant hug. She hopes you feel that hug in these precious words.

Here's to living all the letters in the alphabet!

Made in the USA
Middletown, DE
05 February 2023